Easy Cards
for
All Occasions

Easy Cards

for

All Occasions

Jacquelyn Shenise

STERLING PUBLISHING CO., INC.
NEW YORK

Acknowledgments

I would like to take this opportunity to thank everyone who has encouraged and supported me throughout the years in all my crafting endeavors and who have helped make this book possible.

I would especially like to thank my editor and friend, Danielle Truscott, for her continued expertise and guidance throughout the making of this book.

Dedication

This book is dedicated to Paul for his love and unending devotion. My best friend and the inspiration driving my creativity, he is an endless source of guidance and support. His patience, enthusiasm, and encouragement have made this book possible. Always challenging me to be my best and believing in me when it really mattered, he has helped me make my dreams a reality. For that, I thank him with all my heart.

Photography by Keith Wright/Wright Creative
Design by Kay Shuckhart/Blond on Pond

Library of Congress Cataloging-in-Publication Data

Shenise, Jacquelyn.
  Easy cards for all occasions / Jacquelyn Shenise.
    p. cm.
  Includes index.
  ISBN 1-4027-1230-8
  1. Greeting cards. I. Title.

TT872.B47 2004
745.594'1--dc22

2004019382

10 9 8 7 6 5 4 3 2 1
Published by Sterling Publishing Co., Inc.
387 Park Avenue South, New York, NY 10016
© 2004 by Jacquelyn Shenise
Distributed in Canada by Sterling Publishing
c/o Canadian Manda Group, 165 Dufferin Street
Toronto, Ontario, Canada M6K 3H6
Distributed in Great Britain by Chrysalis Books Group PLC
The Chrysalis Building, Bramley Road, London W10 6SP, England
Distributed in Australia by Capricorn Link (Australia) Pty. Ltd.
P.O. Box 704, Windsor, NSW 2756, Australia

Printed in China
All rights reserved

Sterling ISBN 1-4027-1230-8

Contents

Introduction

Do you love handmade cards? I do. I love to send and receive them, because handmade cards say "I love you" or "I'm thinking of you" in a special way. When you design and make your own cards, your family and friends, your colleagues and neighbors *know* you care! Half the fun of sending a card is making it yourself. Since childhood, I have loved to color, cut, and paste. Card making gives me the opportunity to do those things.

I have been a crafter for many years, and I have tried almost everything at least once. When I discovered the art of card making, I was hooked. I continue to learn, expanding on old techniques and developing new ones.

This book is for everyone—beginners as well as experts. Easy-to-read, step-by-step instructions for all projects provide beginners with the confidence to explore their creativity. Experienced crafters will find fresh and exciting ideas with which to experiment.

The most important thing to keep in mind is having fun. Experiment—make your work unique and make it your own. Use the tools and ideas provided and run with them. Change colors or stamp choices to suit your personal preferences; let your creativity flow!

General Instructions

- The projects in this book are organized according to difficulty. At each level, you will learn new techniques and skills and then build on them in subsequent projects.

- Before beginning a project, make sure to:
    * Read the "Materials & Tools" and "Techniques" chapters.
    * Read the instructions.
    * Gather all materials and tools.

- The patterns for all the projects are in the back of the book. You can transfer patterns very easily.
    * Trace the pattern onto tracing paper.
    * Position the tracing paper on your card and tape it down to hold it in place.
    * Slide a piece of graphite paper underneath the tracing paper.
    * Trace over the pattern with a stylus. This will transfer the pattern lightly to your card. If you are using vellum for your project, work right on the vellum by placing the pattern underneath and tracing lightly.

- Another alternative after tracing the pattern onto tracing paper is to:
    * Cut out the pattern from the tracing paper.
    * Place it on your card and secure it with tape.
    * Trace around the edges of the pattern lightly so the outline shows on your project.

- If you cannot find preprinted, patterned paper that is just right for your project, make your own. It's easy. For making striped papers, use a chisel-edge marker, a fine-line marker, or a combination of both. Using a ruler, draw a series of lines until the paper is covered. Large background stamps are also excellent for making patterned paper. Just stamp until the paper is covered. You can also use small design stamps and repeat the pattern until the paper is covered. For an added effect, try embossing the design (see Chapter 3). Whatever method you choose, be sure to cover the entire sheet of paper. Cut what you need for your card and save the rest for another project.

- Greetings and instructions for making them are located in Chapter 7.

TIPS FOR SUCCESS

- Always practice rubber stamping on scrap paper first. You will get a feel for stamping and avoid wasting good paper.

- Test all markers, colored pencils, pens, paint, etc., on scrap paper. You will want to know exact colors, the amount of bleeding, and mixing properties before starting.

- Stickers can be substituted for rubber-stamped images and original artwork. Stickers are an excellent source of artwork—and can save time.

- Use large rubber stamps to make great background designs and create your own patterned papers.

- Vary the kinds of papers you choose for your projects. Use watercolor, textured, and construction paper (heavy stocks) instead of plain card stock. That will give your cards more texture.

- Pay attention to the weights of the papers you select. Use heavier weights to build your cards and lighter weights to embellish them.

- Do not use permanent markers on rubber stamps. The ink will stain them.

- Before making any cuts, be sure you have read the directions and know how many images you will need from each sheet of paper.

- You can use prepackaged cards and envelopes instead of cutting your own cards from sheets of card stock.

- Raise any image by placing foam tape underneath it instead of gluing it flat.

- Use the same stamps for more than one project. You don't need to buy a large number of rubber stamps to get started.

- Cut out and save images from magazines and coloring books to work into your designs.

- Interchange markers and colored pencils or use them together.

- Enhance that personal touch: Stamp or hand-letter your name on the backs of your cards.

- When selecting rubber stamps for a project, try to purchase stamps similar in theme, shape, and size. If sizes vary too much, you may have to alter the size of your card.

- Select a greeting and decide where to put it before you start a project.

CHAPTER TWO

Materials & Tools

This section will help you select your materials and tools and explain the uses for each. It will help you decide which items will work best for you as well as spark creative ideas to enhance all your card-making projects.

PAPER

Paper is probably the most important material for card making. Always be on the lookout for eye-catching textures, colors, prints, patterns, and weights. Try to select as wide a variety of papers as possible. Interesting papers make interesting cards.

Some of the more common types of paper are card stock, construction paper, drawing paper, watercolor paper, charcoal paper, art paper, vellum, mulberry paper, tissue paper, foil paper, handmade paper, wrapping paper, scratch paper, and paper bags. Don't limit yourself to what you find in the paper section of the craft store. Search everywhere. Every scrap of paper is potential card material.

When choosing an appropriate paper, weight is very important. **Heavy papers**, such as **card stock, construction paper**, and **watercolor paper**, are excellent choices for the card itself. Lighter weights may not support embellishments properly and are usually better to use for the designs on the card.

Varying the sizes of your cards is good. Each card should be unique. Making a card larger or smaller may enhance its design. Never throw out scraps. Even small pieces may be useful—they're great for making collages. Small scraps of paper I have stumbled on by accident have inspired many designs.

Collect as many different colors and patterns as you can. You never know where they will fit in. Try using **leftover wrapping paper** or a piece of **brown grocery bag**. **Tissue paper** can add a different effect to a project. Look for **textured papers**; they can really give your cards an exciting look. Don't limit yourself when it comes to paper; experiment with everything you find. Remember the most important step: Have fun.

SCISSORS, PAPER EDGERS, CRAFT KNIVES, AND PAPER CUTTERS

Cutting tools are a must for making cards. Try to obtain as many as possible. To start, you need good, sharp cutting **scissors**—a large pair for the big stuff and a small pair for the details.

Paper edgers come in a variety of decorative designs and are excellent for adding special touches. You can use them in many ways. Create decorative edges along the sides of a card or cut out shapes to paste on your card.

A good **craft knife** is a must. Always keep sharp blades on hand so your cuts stay crisp. This tool is perfect for cutting out windows, trimming artwork, and adding small details. Buy a self-healing rubber mat to use as a cutting surface. It's a perfect accessory for working with craft knives.

Paper cutters come in a variety of shapes and sizes. There are small and large straight trimmers for making the main cuts and all other straight cuts. Circle and oval cutters make cutting those shapes easy. Try rotary cutters to add decorative edges to your pieces. Buy extra blades and interchange them to make a variety of patterns. It's a good idea to have at least one or two of these cutting implements. They are real timesavers and make extremely accurate cuts.

RULERS

You need a good ruler for measuring and using as a cutting edge. A wood or plastic ruler is fine for measuring, but you'll want a ruler with a **metal edge** for cutting. You could cut a **wood** or **plastic** ruler with your craft knife and chip away at your straightedge.

GLUE

Adhesives come in many forms. A few good ones to have on hand are a **glue stick, white glue, rubber cement,** and a **glue gun** (for hot gluing). These should cover most of your gluing needs. The glue stick is good for

joining light items, such as papers, and dries very quickly. Rubber cement and white glue are good choices for slightly heavier items—such as foam, felt, or fabric—and light embellishments. Heavy items—such as silk flowers, butterflies, metal, wood, plaster, or plastic embellishments—stay put best if you use hot glue. Keep an assortment of glues on hand, especially if you use a variety of materials and embellishments on your cards.

CORRUGATORS

A corrugator, or crimper, is a handy tool for adding another dimension to the design of your cards. Running a sheet of card stock through the corrugator will give your paper a nice rippling effect. Incorporate it into layers of paper for a three-dimensional look. Try positioning the ripples vertically and horizontally to enhance your design and produce different effects.

PUNCHES

A variety of punches, from **handheld** to **square punches**, are available and have many uses. A **hand-**

held rectangular punch makes small holes in a card for stringing cord and ribbon. **Shape punches** are great for making your own die cuts. When punching out shapes from a sheet of paper, do not discard the paper—use it for a background design to mount on your card. You might also save it for making another card or a collage. **Corner rounders** and punches add different shapes to your corners, giving the card a unique look. Punches can be a lot of fun to use. Try them all!

MARKERS, COLORED PENCILS, PASTELS, AND PAINT

Color is an important design element, and experimenting with a variety of mediums can be fun and exciting.

Markers and **colored pencils** are good choices for coloring in rubber-stamped images. Markers will give you a more vibrant color scheme; colored pencils will result in a more pastel palette. Use them for making stripes on solid background papers, adding details such as swirls or flowers, or just lettering a greeting.

To add subtle splashes of color here and there, try using **pastels**. They come in a variety of colors and forms. Stick pastels are easy to use; just color with them. Pastels also come in trays. Use a makeup applicator, cotton swab, or cotton ball with a dab of chalk to create a light, delicate glow of color.

For foam stamps, **paint** is an excellent choice. **Acrylics** provide the best coverage, can be mixed to the exact shade desired, and dry quickly. Use more than one color in the same design to add variety. Acrylics and **oils** are the best choices for painting original artwork. Mix them to create the desired effect.

Watercolor is perfect for creating a light and airy design either freehand or from a rubber-stamped image. **Watercolor pencils** let you create a watercolor appearance without all the mess. They are easy to work with and usually produce a very desirable result. Watercolors and watercolor pencils, acrylics, and oils are readily available in most art and craft stores. Experiment with various mediums until you find the one that suits the

particular project and your taste and that you can work with comfortably at your skill level.

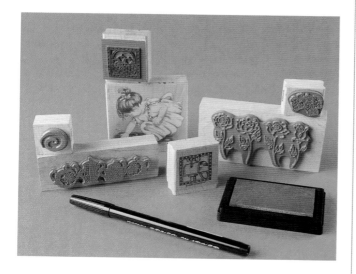

RUBBER STAMPS AND STAMP PADS

Rubber stamps can be among your most versatile tools. You can find them in craft and stationery stores. Use stamps to create designs ranging from fun to elegant. A **large picture stamp** can provide the main artwork and focus of a card. You can create a great background with either a **large background stamp** or a **small design stamp** repeated over an entire sheet of paper. The possibilities are endless.

For working with rubber stamps, you will need to purchase a few **stamp pads**. Select stamp pads that are on the wet side. If a pad is too dry, stamping an image can be difficult. A dry stamp pad will sometimes produce a lighter image. **Multicolor stamp pads** offer an easy way of adding multiple colors and a different look.

Markers make a great alternative or addition to stamp pads for use with rubber stamps. They are not as messy and dry faster. Markers allow you to use several colors on the stamp with control.

Collect as many different stamps, pads, and markers as possible and experiment. As you do, you will learn which pads and markers work best with which stamps and which work best for you.

ROLLERS

Rollers come in a variety of sizes, shapes, and styles, depending on your craft needs. Some rollers have **interchangeable rubber stamp rolls** for stamping background designs on larger areas.

Rubber rollers are excellent for applying paint to foam rubber stamps. Rolling the paint on the foam stamp can create a smooth or textured effect. **Foam rollers** are another alternative. Rollers offer a fun and easy way of creating special effects with paint. It is a good idea to have at least one type of roller on hand.

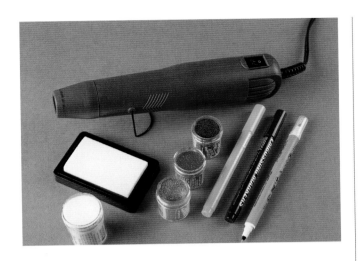

EMBOSSING TOOLS

Embossing adds another dimension to any card, allowing you to obtain a variety of looks and enhance the design. The most important tool is the **embossing stamp pad**. A good pad is essential for a good outcome. Two types are available: pre-inked and un-inked. If you choose a pre-inked pad, make sure you buy a good wet one. Keep an un-inked pad well inked and wet.

Embossing powders are available in many colors and styles. You can purchase **glitters** for adding a sparkle. Experiment with as many powders in as wide a color range as you can.

An **embossing pen** is a must for writing. Embossing pens can be purchased with multiple tips, such as a fine point, a broad point, or a calligraphy point. Use an embossing pen to write greetings, personalize your work, highlight artwork, or add accents here and there. Because these pens have no color, you will need to apply **colored powders** over them. **Colored embossing pens** are another option and provide a great and easy way to emboss in color.

When using colored pens, markers, or stamp pads, you will need a bottle of **clear embossing powder** because the color is already there. This is a fun way to enhance a picture.

The last item you will need is an **embossing gun**, or **heat tool**, which you can pick up in most craft stores. This will melt the embossing powder to give your image a raised effect.

EMBELLISHMENTS

You can find embellishments almost anywhere. Just about anything smaller than your card is potential material. Consider items found in bags of potpourri, silk flowers (clip off the stems), dried flowers, leaves, butterflies, buttons, decorative ornaments, wood cutouts, and beads.

Three-dimensional stickers are available in every theme imaginable and add fun to your designs. Stickers have great artwork and are very easy to work with. Once you start looking for embellishments, you'll be surprised at the number of ideas you'll get.

Techniques

In this section, you'll find explanations of the various techniques used throughout the book. You will learn to use the materials and tools for everything from simple cutting and pasting to more difficult and advanced techniques, such as embossing. Gather your tools and let's practice!

CUTTING AND PASTING

Cutting and pasting is the first technique you need to learn. It is also the most commonly used and the easiest to master.

For most of the projects in this book, the design includes layering multiple sheets of paper. You may want to substitute colors, textures, styles, prints, and the number of layers to suit your taste. Always remember to vary your papers. Try mixing textured papers with smooth papers or prints with solids. If you prefer a different color on your card, don't let the suggested color selections limit you.

When adding layers of paper, try to keep border sizes consistent. A good combination to try is ⅛-inch borders on all layers. If you want a larger colored border, try ⅛-inch on the first layer, ½-inch on the second layer, and ⅛-inch on the third layer. That will make the middle color more dominant. Laying the papers out to try different border sizes before gluing is always a good idea.

Double-sided foam tape works well for adding a little dimension to the layers. Use the tape to raise one or more layers—or all of them!

CUTTING WINDOWS

Making windows is a simple technique for enhancing your work. Cutting a window in a card gives it a three-dimensional appearance. Follow these steps to successfully cut windows:

• Measure carefully before cutting.

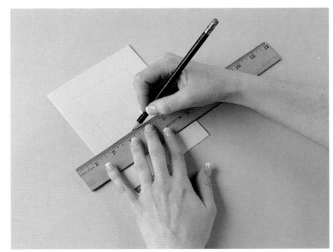

- Lightly mark the window outline with a pencil.
- Use a metal or metal-edged ruler.
- Always cut along the edge of the ruler for accuracy with a craft knife.
- Position the image behind the window.

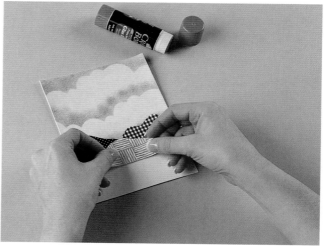

MAKING COLLAGES

Anything goes when it comes to collage. Collect as many different kinds of papers and embellishments as you can get your hands on. Also keep a variety of glues on hand. Different items will require different types of glue.

The first step is selecting the materials. Try to mix the textures, prints, and colors for a more interesting and striking collage. Papers preprinted with clouds, trees, grass, mountains, and flowers work great in landscape collages. Do not overuse these papers; include some shapes cut from solid and patterned papers as well. Add embellishments for that multidimensional look.

Once you assemble your materials, cut out all the

shapes you plan to use. Arrange them on your card before gluing to make sure you are satisfied with the layout.

USING RUBBER STAMPS

Rubber stamps can provide a great source of artwork for all your projects. Many different kinds of stamps are available in craft stores. You will need to purchase a few markers and stamp pads to use with your stamps. Here are some stamping basics:

Markers

- Color a rubber stamp with a black marker (not permanent), making sure to ink it well.
- Carefully position the stamp on the paper and press firmly.
- Gently lift the stamp from the paper.
- Let the image dry thoroughly, and color in the design with markers, colored pencils, etc.

Stamp Pads

- Press the stamp into the stamp pad, inking well.
- Position the stamp on the paper and press firmly.
- Lift the stamp from the paper.
- Let the image dry thoroughly, and color it if you like.

Using these techniques, you can create a variety of effects, depending on the stamps you select. Stamps with a lot of detail can be left with just a black outline or colored in. For stamps that have large, flat, bold areas, you can add color to the stamp with markers or use with a multicolor stamp pad.

When working with foam stamps, acrylic paint is an excellent choice. Place the paint on a sheet of wax

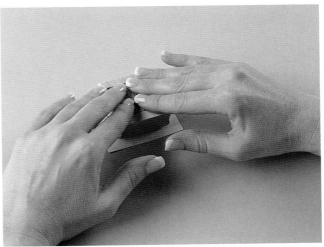

paper. Using a rubber roller, roll over the paint until it covers the roller evenly and thoroughly. Roll one more time on a clean sheet of wax paper just to make sure the paint is even and not too thick. Then roll the paint onto the stamp and carefully position the stamp on your paper. Press gently, being careful not to rock the stamp back and forth. Lift the stamp slowly from the paper and let it dry.

Watermark stamp pads are readily available in most craft stores. A stamp used with a watermark pad leaves an impression slightly darker than the paper, similar to a watermark. This technique is especially useful when working on darker papers, where stamping with dark markers would not be visible.

EMBOSSING

Embossing can add a very special look to your projects and is another fairly easy technique. Projects in this book require four basic methods.

Clear Embossing Pad with Colored Powders

- Press a rubber stamp firmly into a clear embossing pad.
- Position it on the paper and press firmly.
- Lift the stamp and set it aside; the image will be barely visible.
- Sprinkle colored embossing powder generously over the entire image.
- Pour off the excess powder.
- Heat the image with the embossing gun, slowly working from side to side. Do not overheat.

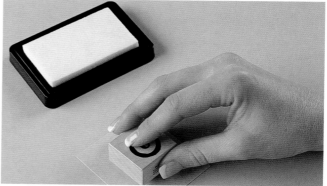

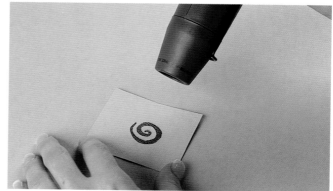

Colored Markers and Stamp Pads with Clear Powder

- Color a rubber stamp or press it into a colored stamp pad.
- Position the stamp on the paper and press firmly.
- Lift the stamp and set it to the side.
- Sprinkle clear embossing powder generously over the entire image.
- Pour off the excess powder.
- Heat the image with the embossing gun, slowly working from side to side. Do not overheat.

Clear Embossing Pen with Colored Powder (for writing)

- Transfer or trace an image or lettering onto the project.
- Carefully trace over the image or lettering with the embossing pen.
- Sprinkle colored embossing powder generously over the entire image.
- Pour off the excess powder.

- Heat the image with the embossing gun, slowly working from side to side. Do not overheat.

Colored Embossing Pens with Clear Powder

- Stamp the image to be embossed on your paper and let it dry.
- Working in small sections, begin coloring the image with embossing pens.
- Sprinkle clear embossing powder generously over the colored area.
- Pour off the excess powder
- Heat the image with the embossing gun, slowly working from side to side. Do not overheat.

Don't throw away used embossing powders; you can use them again! Keep clean sheets of paper handy to hold used powder until you can return it to the jar. Always practice embossing techniques on a piece of scrap paper before trying them on your project.

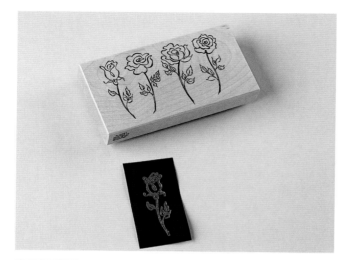

USING SCRATCH PAPER

Scratch paper can be purchased in most craft stores and is ready to use. You can select black with gold, silver, or multicolor underneath or white with color underneath. For the projects in this book, I chose black with multicolor underneath.

The most important part of this technique is selecting which rubber stamp to use. You want a stamp that will accentuate and utilize the colors of the paper. Stamps with detailed outlines and large open areas are good choices. Themes such as flowers, windows, and scenery usually work well. Follow these simple steps to work with scratch paper:

- Select the rubber stamp.
- Ink the stamp on a clear embossing pad.
- Press onto the scratch paper.
- Emboss with gold embossing powder.
- Using a wooden stylus, scratch out the large areas where you want the color to show through.

Mounting your design on white or light-colored paper will make the colors look more brilliant. Experiment with backgrounds of different colors before gluing.

USING WATERCOLOR PENCILS

Watercolor pencils are a neat and easy alternative to watercolor paint. There are just a few simple steps to this technique:

- Stamp an image with a rubber stamp and let it dry thoroughly.

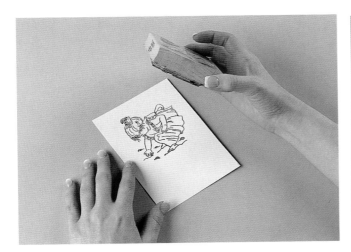

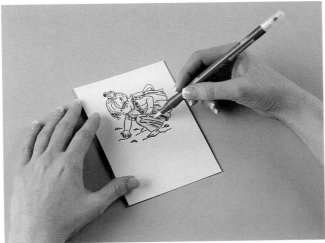

- Using the pencils, place small dabs of color at the edges of the areas to be painted.
- Use a blender pen carefully to pull the color from an edge into the center.
- If you want more color, color more with the pencils; if you want less color, use the blender pen more.

USING STICKERS

Stickers can be a great resource for artwork and embellishments. You can also substitute stickers for any of the small rubber stamps used in this book. Stickers are very popular and found in almost all craft stores. If you cannot find exactly what you want, make your own. These two simple sticker-making techniques will come in handy in your card-making projects:

Technique 1

- Rubber-stamp or transfer any image onto white card stock and color as desired.
- Cover the completed image with a laminating sheet.
- Trim around the edges, leaving a slight overhang for attaching your sticker.

Technique 2

- Rubber-stamp or trace any image directly onto the laminating sheet; let it dry thoroughly.
- Color the image with permanent markers; let it dry thoroughly.
- Use a craft knife to cut out the image.
- Peel off the backing, and place the image on your project.

Beginner-Level Projects

You have learned about materials, tools, and techniques. Now you are ready to begin your first project. This section starts you off with easy card designs that involve the smallest number of materials, techniques, and steps. This is a great starting point for your first attempt at card making. So gather your tools and let's get started.

Rose Garden

A cheerful foam rose is the star of this colorful garden. It says "Happy Birthday," "Get Well," or simply "Hello." You might want to use preprinted flower paper to create the background image for your card.

Card Size: 5 × 6½ inches

Materials

- one 8½ × 11-inch sheet cream card stock
- one 8½ × 11-inch sheet yellow card stock
- one 8½ × 11-inch sheet white card stock
- one 8½ × 11-inch sheet lime green card stock
- one 8½ × 11-inch sheet bright blue card stock
- Rose Garden pattern (page 110)
- scraps of yellow and green foam

Tools

- scissors
- ruler
- glue
- flower rubber stamp for background image or a sheet of flowered paper
- black stamp pad or marker
- colored pencils

Instructions

1. Cut a piece of cream card stock 6½ × 10 inches and fold in half. The card will measure 5 × 6½ inches with the fold on the left side.

2. Cut a piece of yellow card stock 5 × 6½ inches and glue it to the front of the cream card.

3. Use the rubber stamp to cover the sheet of white card stock with flowers. When the ink is completely dry, use colored pencils to add accents of color to the flowers. Cut a 3 × 4½-inch piece to use as a background image. Mount the background image on a piece of lime green card stock ⅛ inch larger on all sides than the image.

4. Mount the lime green sheet on the remaining piece of yellow card stock, leaving a ½-inch border all around.

5. Mount the yellow sheet on a bright blue sheet, leaving a ⅛-inch border all around.

6. Mount the bright blue sheet on the front of the covered card.

7. Use the rose pattern to cut a rosebud from the yellow foam and the leaves and stem from the green foam. Using the photo as a guide, glue the pieces of the rose to the front of the card over the stamped image.

8. Add the greeting of your choice.

Art Deco

Contrasting tan and black blocks make this "crafty"-looking card a classic. Substituting bright colors for neutrals will make a bold and brilliant statement.

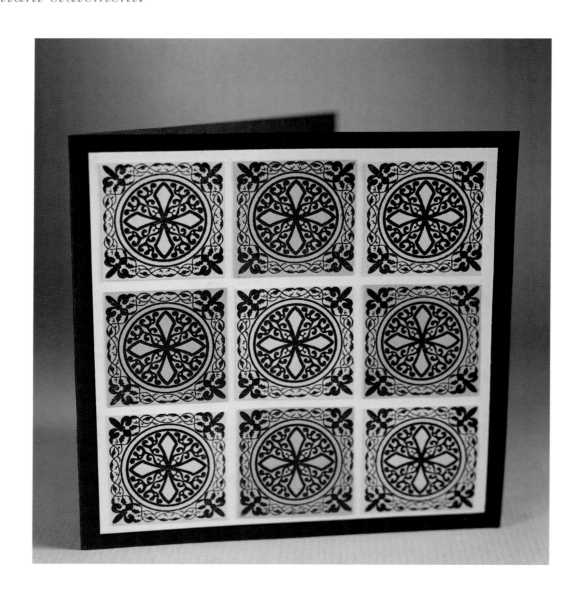

Card Size: 5½ × 5½ inches

Materials

- one 8½ × 11-inch sheet black card stock
- one 8½ × 11-inch sheet tan card stock
- one 8½ × 11-inch sheet cream card stock
- one 8½ × 11-inch sheet white card stock

Tools

- scissors
- ruler
- glue
- patterned rubber stamp, approximately 1½ inches square
- black stamp pad or marker

Instructions

1. Cut a 5½ × 11-inch piece of black card stock. Fold it in half so the card measures 5½ × 5½ inches. This design allows you the choice of opening the card from the top or the side.

2. Using a black stamp pad or marker, stamp the square image four times on the tan card stock and five times on the cream card stock.

3. Cut out the nine square images and glue onto the white card stock. Arrange squares in three rows of three so the cream squares are in the corners and the middle. Leave a ⅛-inch border around all nine squares. If your stamp is larger than 1½ inches square, you will need to increase the size of the black card.

4. Center the white card stock on the front of the black card and glue in place.

5. Add the greeting of your choice.

Potpourri

This fanciful collage can suit any taste, depending on the potpourri pieces you choose. Shapes, textures, and colors are the key to this design, so let your imagination go wild.

Card Size: 6 × 6 inches

Materials

- one 6 × 12-inch sheet light green textured paper
- brown paint
- potpourri leaves and berries

Tools

- scissors
- ruler
- assorted leaf rubber stamps
- stamp pads and markers in greens, browns, and reds
- stylus
- glue

Instructions

1. Fold the light green textured paper in half so the card measures 6 × 6 inches with the fold on the left side.

2. Using the assorted leaf stamps, begin covering the front of the card with leaf images in shades of green, brown, and red. To make the card more interesting, try using more than one color on some of the leaves.

3. Lightly dip the stylus or the end of a paintbrush handle in the brown paint and dot the card in between the leaf images, making a spotted pattern. Reload paint when dots become light.

4. Select a few pieces from the bag of potpourri. Arrange in an eye-catching design and glue to the card.

5. Add the greeting of your choice.

Window of Spring

Capture the beauty of spring with the simplicity of watercolors. This delicate-looking card is appropriate for almost any occasion and is ready for framing.

Card Size: 6 × 6 inches

Materials

- one 6 × 12-inch sheet watercolor paper

Tools

- scissors
- ruler
- craft knife
- flower rubber stamp
- grass rubber stamp
- markers in a variety of colors, including green

Instructions

1. Fold the watercolor paper in half. The card will measure 6 × 6 inches with the fold at the top.

2. Using a craft knife, cut a 2 × 2-inch square opening. Position the opening 1 inch from the top and 2 inches from each side.

3. With the markers, color the flower rubber stamp, using any color of your choice on the flower and green on the stem.

4. Stamp one flower image on the bottom right of the card front. Stamp strands of grass at the bottom of the flower image. If a grass stamp is not available, use a fine green marker and add a few blades around the base of the stem.

5. Stamp three flower images on the inside of the card, positioning them so they show through the window.

6. Add the greeting of your choice.

Dorothy's Best

Dorothy's best pink dress is perfect for that special young woman as she approaches her prom, graduation, or sweet-sixteen celebration. Your thoughtfulness will delight her.

Card Size: $4^{3}/_{4} \times 5^{3}/_{8}$ inches

Materials

- two $8^{1}/_{2} \times 11$-inch sheets white card stock
- one $8^{1}/_{2} \times 11$-inch sheet pink card stock
- one $8^{1}/_{2} \times 11$-inch sheet black card stock

Tools

- scissors
- ruler
- dress rubber stamp
- black stamp pad or marker
- light pink colored pencil

Instructions

1. Cut a $5^{3}/_{8} \times 9^{1}/_{2}$-inch piece of white card stock. Fold in half so the card measures $4^{3}/_{4} \times 5^{3}/_{8}$ inches with the fold at the top.

2. Cut a $3^{7}/_{8} \times 3^{1}/_{4}$-inch piece of white card stock. Stamp the dress image in the center. Lightly color in the dress with the light pink pencil.

3. Mount the image on pink card stock, trimming to leave a $^{1}/_{8}$-inch border. Mount on black card stock, leaving a $^{1}/_{4}$-inch border. Mount on pink card stock, leaving a $^{1}/_{8}$-inch border. Glue the completed image to the center of the card, leaving a $^{1}/_{8}$-inch border.

4. Add the greeting of your choice.

Mystical Wizard

Use the mystical wizard to convey an enchanting greeting and magical wishes to that special someone. This colorful card is sure to bring a smile to anyone's face.

Card Size: 5 × 6½ inches

Materials

- two 8½ × 11-inch sheets white card stock
- one 8½ × 11-inch sheet lavender card stock
- one 8½ × 11-inch sheet medium purple card stock
- one 8½ × 11-inch sheet dark purple card stock

Tools

- scissors
- ruler
- wizard rubber stamp
- black stamp pad or marker
- assorted colored pencils
- glue

Instructions

1. Cut a 6½ × 10-inch piece of white card stock. Fold in half so the card measures 5 × 6½ inches with the fold on the left side.

2. Using a black stamp pad or marker, stamp the wizard image on the remaining sheet of white card stock.

3. Color the wizard image with colored pencils. Use the photo as a guide for the colors. (If your stamp has a color image printed on the handle, you can use it as a guide.)

4. Mount the wizard on the lavender card stock, trimming to leave a ⅛-inch border. Mount on the medium purple card stock, leaving a ⅛-inch border. Mount on the dark purple card stock, leaving a ⅛-inch border.

5. Glue the entire image to the front of the card, making sure to center the image.

6. Add the greeting of your choice.

Snow Angel

This timeless classic is the perfect holiday greeting. Elegant, yet simple to create, it's sure to be welcomed by everyone on your holiday list.

Card Size: 5½ × 7 inches

Materials

- one 8½ × 11-inch sheet blue card stock
- white acrylic paint
- sheet of wax paper

Tools

- scissors
- rubber roller
- angel foam stamp

Instructions

1. Cut blue card stock to measure 7 × 11 inches. Fold in half so it measures 5½ × 7 inches with the fold at the top of the card.

2. Pour some white acrylic paint on the wax paper. Coat the rubber roller completely and evenly by rolling it back and forth over the paint-coated wax paper. Apply to the foam stamp.

3. Press the foam stamp evenly on the front of the card.

4. Add the greeting of your choice.

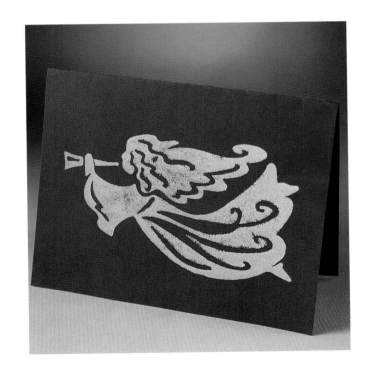

Fruitful Bounty

A basketful of apples is the center of attention in this harvest-themed note card. Congratulate a new homeowner by sharing the bounty.

Card Size: $5\frac{3}{4} \times 6\frac{1}{8}$ inches

Materials

- one $8\frac{1}{2} \times 11$-inch sheet dark red card stock
- one small square white card stock, about $1\frac{1}{2} \times 1\frac{1}{2}$ inches
- one $8\frac{1}{2} \times 11$-inch sheet light brown card stock
- one $8\frac{1}{2} \times 11$-inch sheet dark green card stock
- one 12-inch piece of gold cord

Tools

- scissors
- ruler
- apple-basket rubber stamp, about 1 inch square
- black stamp pad or marker
- markers in a variety of colors
- glue
- corrugater
- paper edgers
- rectangular hole punch

Instructions

1. Cut a $5\frac{3}{4} \times 11$-inch piece of dark red card stock. Fold so that the back of the card is $1\frac{1}{2}$ inches longer than the front. (See photo.)

2. Stamp the basket image on the white card stock. Use markers to color the image. Mount the image on a piece of dark red card stock, trimming to leave a $\frac{1}{8}$-inch border.

3. Cut two squares from the sheet of light brown card stock, one $4\frac{1}{2} \times 4\frac{1}{2}$ inches and the other $2\frac{7}{8} \times 2\frac{7}{8}$ inches. Corrugate both squares. (See Chapter 2.)

4. Mount the completed piece from step 2 in the center of the smaller of the corrugated squares so that the ridges run vertically. Mount on dark green card stock, leaving a $\frac{1}{8}$-inch border. Mount in the center of the larger corrugated square so that the ridges run horizontally. Mount on the front of the card.

5. Cut a $1\frac{1}{2} \times 5\frac{3}{4}$-inch strip of dark green paper. Using the paper edgers, cut a $\frac{1}{4}$-inch strip off lengthwise. You will have two strips, each with a straight edge and a decorative edge. Using the photo as a guide, glue the narrower strip to the inside of the back of the card, about $\frac{1}{4}$ inch from the bottom. Glue the wider strip underneath the front of the card so that about $\frac{3}{4}$ of an inch shows. The dark red should be visible between the dark green strips and on the bottom edge of the card.

6. Punch two rectangular holes in the top of the card, $\frac{1}{4}$ inch from the top and $1\frac{7}{8}$ inches from each side. String the gold cord through the holes and tie a bow. Trim as desired.

7. Add the greeting of your choice.

A Letter from Home

Let that special friend know how much you care with a letter from home. Use it to say "Hello" or "Thank You," send birthday greetings, or announce your new address.

Card Size: 4¼ × 5½ inches

Materials

- one 8½ × 11-inch sheet light brown card stock
- one 8½ × 11-inch sheet light yellow paper
- one 8½ × 11-inch sheet dark brown paper
- small piece white card stock

Tools

- scissors
- ruler
- background rubber stamp with text
- black stamp pad or marker
- mailbox rubber stamp, approximately 1¼ inches square, or a small mailbox sticker
- colored pencils
- glue

Instructions

1. Cut a 5½ × 8½-inch piece of light brown card stock. Fold in half so the card measures 4¼ × 5½ inches with the fold at the top.

2. Using the background stamp and a black stamp pad, stamp the image so that it covers the entire front of the card. Let dry thoroughly.

3. Stamp the mailbox image on the white card stock and trim around image. Color the image with colored pencils. If you prefer, use a sticker (approximately 1¼ × 1¼ inches) in place of the stamped image.

Mount on yellow paper, leaving a ⅛-inch border. Mount on dark brown paper, leaving a ⅜-inch border. Mount on yellow paper, again leaving a ⅛-inch border.

4. Glue the completed image to the center of the front of the card.

5. Add the greeting of your choice.

Holiday Tree

This classic holiday greeting is quick and easy to whip up. An elegant golden tree graces the front of the card. Send everyone you know a special holiday wish!

Card Size: 5 × 6¾ inches

Materials

- one 8½ × 11-inch sheet dark green card stock
- one 3 × 3-inch sheet white card stock
- one 8½ × 11-inch sheet gold paper

Tools

- scissors
- ruler
- tree rubber stamp or gold sticker
- gold stamp pad
- glue

Instructions

1. Cut a 6¾ × 8½-inch piece of dark green card stock. Fold so the back is 1⅝ inches longer than the front and the fold is at the top.

2. Using the gold stamp pad, stamp the tree image on the piece of white card stock. Let it dry thoroughly—metallic ink takes longer to dry and if you touch it too soon, it will smear. Use a sticker if you prefer. Tear the edges until the image measures approximately 2 × 2½ inches. Mount on gold paper, leaving a ¼-inch border. Glue the completed image in the center of the card, leaving room for a gold strip along the bottom. (See photo for placement.)

3. Cut three ¼ × 6½-inch strips from the gold paper. Glue one to the back of the card ⅛ inch from the bottom, glue the second ⅛ inch above the first, and glue the third on the front of the card under the gold image.

4. Add the greeting of your choice.

In the Pink

Bright and colorful is the motif for this cheery greeting. Send it for a birthday, for an anniversary, to offer congratulations, or just to say "Hello." It's sure to put anyone in the pink!

Card Size: $4\frac{1}{2} \times 6\frac{1}{4}$ inches

Materials

- one $8\frac{1}{2} \times 11$-inch sheet white card stock
- one $8\frac{1}{2} \times 11$-inch sheet pink striped paper
- one $8\frac{1}{2} \times 11$-inch sheet glossy white paper
- one $8\frac{1}{2} \times 11$-inch sheet pink plaid paper
- one $8\frac{1}{2} \times 11$-inch sheet pink card stock

Tools

- scissors
- ruler
- glue
- flower rubber stamp
- pink stamp pad

Instructions

1. Cut a $6\frac{1}{4} \times 9$-inch piece of white card stock. Fold in half so the card measures $4\frac{1}{2} \times 6\frac{1}{4}$ inches and the fold is at the top.

2. Cut a $6\frac{1}{4} \times 4\frac{1}{2}$-inch piece of pink striped paper and glue to the front of the card. The stripes should run vertically.

3. Cut a 3×4-inch piece of glossy white paper. Using the pink stamp pad, stamp three flower images on the paper. Let it dry thoroughly.

4. Mount the stamped image on the pink plaid paper, leaving a $\frac{1}{4}$-inch border. Mount on the pink card stock, leaving a $\frac{1}{8}$-inch border. Center the completed image on the front of the card and glue.

5. Add the greeting of your choice

Bundle of Joy

These cuddly little bears are a perfect way of announcing that special new arrival. Personalize the card with the baby's name and frame it for the nursery.

Card Size: 5 × 6½ inches

Materials

- one 8½ × 11-inch sheet white card stock
- one 8½ × 11-inch sheet yellow card stock
- one 8½ × 11-inch sheet light pink card stock
- one 8½ × 11-inch sheet light blue card stock

Tools

- scissors
- ruler
- glue
- teddy-bear rubber stamp, about 1¼ inches square
- colored pencils
- double-sided foam tape

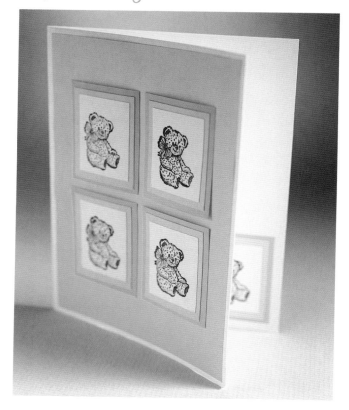

Instructions

1. Cut a 6½ × 10-inch piece of white card stock. Fold in half so the card measures 5 × 6½ inches and the fold is on the left side.

2. Cut a 4¾ × 6¼-inch piece of yellow card stock and glue to the center of the white card, leaving a ⅛-inch border of white.

3. Stamp the teddy bear image on the white card stock five times. Cut a square around each image. Color the bears with colored pencils, alternating the bow colors between blue and pink. (See photo.)

4. Mount each bear on light pink card stock, leaving a ⅛-inch border, and then on blue, leaving a ⅛-inch border. Position two bears with pink bows and two bears with blue bows on the front of the card. Attach with double-sided foam tape for a three-dimensional look. Remember to alternate the pink and blue bows.

5. Glue the last bear image flat inside the card in the bottom right corner.

6. Add the greeting of your choice.

Summertime Fun

This bold party invitation features juicy watermelon wedges. Don't have a summer barbecue without it. Who could resist?

Card Size: 4¼ × 5½ inches

Materials

- one 5½ × 8½-inch sheet glossy white card stock

Tools

- scissors
- assorted watermelon rubber stamps
- red, green, and black markers

Instructions

1. Fold the sheet of glossy white card stock in half so it measures 4¼ × 5½ inches with the fold on the top of the card.

2. Color the watermelon rubber stamp with the red and green markers and stamp in a random pattern on the front of the card. Let dry thoroughly—ink dries more slowly on glossy paper.

3. When completely dry, color in the seeds with the black marker.

4. If you plan to use as a party invitation, you can purchase an invitation stamp to use on the inside, or you can hand-letter your information. If used as a card, select the greeting of your choice.

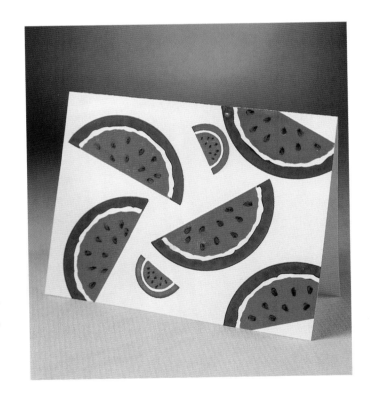

Autumn Splendor

Contrasting fall leaves deliver a special autumn greeting in this three-dimensional card. Use it for notes, to say "I miss you," or for friendship messages.

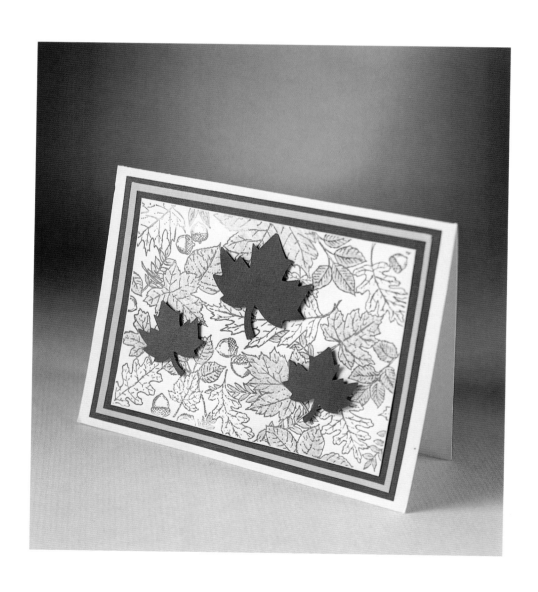

Card Size: 5 × 6½ inches

Materials

- two 8½ × 11-inch sheets white card stock
- one 8½ × 11-inch sheet dark brown card stock
- one 8½ × 11-inch sheet tan card stock

Tools

- scissors
- glue
- background leaf rubber stamp
- multicolor stamp pad in autumn colors
- colored pencils
- leaf-shaped punches
- double-sided foam tape

Instructions

1. Cut a piece of white card stock 6½ × 10 inches. Fold in half so the card measures 5 × 6½ inches with the fold at the top.

2. Press the background rubber stamp on the multicolor stamp pad randomly so different colors ink different areas of the stamp. Stamp the image on a piece of white card stock and trim to 4 × 5¼ inches.

3. Add a color accent by lightly coloring some of the leaves with colored pencils—do not overcolor.

4. Mount on dark brown card stock, leaving a ⅛-inch border. Mount on tan card stock, leaving a ⅛-inch border. Mount on dark brown card stock, leaving a ⅛-inch border. Mount on card front.

5. From the remaining dark brown card stock, punch out several leaves and attach to the front of the card with double-sided foam tape. If you do not have leaf punches, trace leaves from a magazine or coloring book for a pattern. Cut by hand.

6. Add the greeting of your choice.

Festive Announcement

How could anyone refuse this sassy invitation to your next New Year's Eve party? Your guests will be thrilled to be invited. You might send it as a bon voyage wish to friends about to take that long-awaited vacation.

Card Size: 4¼ × 5½ inches

Materials

- Festive Announcement patterns (page 111)
- one 8½ × 11-inch sheet yellow card stock
- one 8½ × 11-inch sheet black dotted paper
- one 8½ × 11-inch sheet black striped paper
- small piece white card stock
- small piece laminating sheet
- tracing paper

Tools

- scissors
- ruler
- glue
- cocktail-glass rubber stamp or stickers
- markers
- craft knife

Instructions

1. Use the pattern to cut the card out of yellow card stock. Fold in half (on the line) and position the card with the fold on the left.

2. Cut the dotted paper in a triangular shape ⅛ inch smaller than the card front and glue in place. Cut the striped paper in a similar triangular shape ⅛ inch smaller than the dotted paper and glue in place. (See photo for placement.)

3. Cut a ¼-inch strip from the dotted paper. Cut to form two 1½-inch strips and two 3¼-inch strips. Glue to the inside top right corner of the card in a rectangu-lar shape. Be sure the yellow of the card is showing through the middle of the rectangle.

4. Stamp the cocktail glass image on white card stock three times. Color in with markers. Place a piece of laminate over each image and carefully cut out the images with a craft knife. Glue one to the outside of the card in the bottom left corner. Glue one on the inside of the card in the bottom right corner. Glue the third one inside the rectangle on the inside of the card. (See photo for placement.) You can use cocktail-glass stickers instead.

5. Add the greeting of your choice.

Intermediate-Level Projects

Now that you have mastered the basic card-making techniques for beginners, you are ready for new challenges. This section will incorporate what you have already learned and add some new techniques. Let's get started!

Daisy Dreams

These delightful daisies will brighten anyone's day. Spread the cheer and let people know you treasure their friendship.

Card Size: 5½ × 7¼ inches

Materials

- one 8½ × 11-inch sheet cream textured paper

Tools

- scissors
- ruler
- assorted flower and leaf rubber stamps
- speckled rubber stamp
- assorted stamp pads and markers

Instructions

1. Cut a 7¼ × 11 inch piece of textured paper. Fold in half so that the card measures 5½ × 7¼ inches and the fold is on the left side.

2. Using the flower and leaf stamps, stamp the design on the card front. (See photo.) Mix up the images and use a variety of colors randomly.

3. Using the speckled stamp and a dark brown stamp pad, lightly stamp over the design until the card front is covered with dots. If you do not have a speckled stamp, you can use a stylus and paint to achieve the same effect.

4. Add the greeting of your choice.

Festival of Color

Send a festival of color as a birthday greeting or a get-well card.
Yellow and pink foam flowers complete the look.

Card Size: 5 × 6½ inches

Materials

- two 8½ × 11-inch sheets cream card stock
- Festival of Color patterns (page 112)
- scraps of yellow, pink, and green foam
- tracing paper

Tools

- scissors
- ruler
- flower rubber stamp
- assorted markers
- glue
- flower punch
- paper edgers

Instructions

1. Cut a piece of cream card stock 6½ × 10 inches. Fold in half so that the card measures 5 × 6½ inches and the fold is on the left.

2. Cut another piece of cream card stock 4¾ × 6½ inches. Using different colored markers and the photo as a guide, color the flower stamp and stamp the card stock until the entire piece is completely covered. Stamp the images off the edges of the paper, as shown.

3. Glue to the card front. Using the edgers, cut a 1-inch strip off the right side of the card front only. Trim the 1-inch strip down to a ¾-inch strip, leaving the decorative edge intact.

4. Open the card and lay flat. Glue the ¾-inch strip to the inside of the card, positioning it to the far right edge. (See photo.)

5. Punch two flowers from yellow and pink foam. If you do not have a flower punch, draw or trace any flower pattern onto the foam and cut by hand. Use the patterns to make stems and leaves from the green foam. Position on the front of the card and glue in place.

6. Add the greeting of your choice.

Fields of Flowers

The garden is in full bloom, ready to make any occasion special. These lovely flowers complement them all.

Card Size: 5⅝ × 7 inches

Materials

- two 8½ × 11-inch sheets white card stock
- one 8½ × 11-inch sheet blue patterned paper
- one 8½ × 11-inch sheet lavender paper
- one 8½ × 11-inch sheet cream paper

Tools

- scissors
- ruler
- glue
- flower rubber stamp
- black stamp pad or marker
- colored pencils

Instructions

1. Cut a piece of white card stock 7 × 10 inches. Fold over 4½ inches of the 10-inch length, leaving the back 1¼ inches wider than the front. The card should measure 5⅝ × 7 inches with the fold on the left side.

2. Cover the front of the card with the blue patterned paper.

3. Open the card and cover the right side with blue patterned paper.

4. Stamp the flower image on a piece of white card stock and trim to size. Color the image with the pencils. Mount on a piece of lavender paper, leaving a ½-inch border.

5. Mount on a piece of cream paper, leaving a ⅛-inch border.

6. Close the card and glue the image to the front, ⅞-inch from the top, bottom, and left sides. The image will hang over the right edge of the card front.

7. Add the greeting of your choice.

Victorian Valentine

Show your special someone you care with this rich, golden valentine of love. Personalize the gold heart for an added touch.

Card Size: 5 × 5⅜ inches

Materials

- one 8½ × 11-inch sheet pink card stock
- one 8½ × 11-inch sheet vellum
- small paper gold heart doily
- small sheet gold paper
- gold embossing powder

Tools

- scissors
- ruler
- glue
- small heart rubber stamp
- clear embossing pad
- embossing gun

Instructions

1. Cut a piece of pink card stock 5⅜ × 8½ inches. Fold 3½ inches of the 8½-inch length so that the card back is 1½ inches longer than the front. The card should measure 5 × 5⅜ inches with the fold at the top.

2. Cover the front of the card with vellum. Stamp the small heart randomly on the vellum and emboss. (See page 20, "Embossing.")

3. Using the photo as a guide, glue the heart doily to the front of the card. The doily will hang over the edge.

4. Cut two ¼-inch strips of gold paper. Glue the first strip to the card back ¼ inch from the bottom. Glue the second strip ¼ inch above the first. (See photo.)

5. Add the greeting of your choice.

A Crisp Morning

Raffia complements the handmade paper used in this card, and a multicolor stamp pad heightens the effect of autumn leaves.

Card Size: 5 × 6½ inches

Materials

- one 8½ × 11-inch sheet white card stock
- one 8½ × 11-inch sheet handmade paper in a neutral shade
- one 8½ × 11-inch sheet vellum
- one 20-inch piece of raffia

Tools

- scissors
- ruler
- glue
- leaf rubber stamp
- multicolor stamp pad
- rectangular hole punch

Instructions

1. Cut a piece of white card stock 6¼ × 9¾ inches. Fold in half so the card measures 4⅞ × 6¼ inches and the fold is on the left side.

2. Open the card and lay it out flat. Cover the entire outside of card with a 6¼ × 9¾-inch piece of handmade paper.

3. Cut a piece of vellum 6½ × 10 inches and fold in half to cover the entire card. Using the multicolor stamp pad, thoroughly ink the leaf stamp. Move the pad around so that the colors mix and overlap on the stamp. Stamp two leaf images on the front of the vellum.

4. Place vellum over the card so the leaf images are on the front of the card.

5. Punch two rectangular holes in the fold of the card, ½ inch from the top and ½ inch from the bottom.

6. String the raffia through the holes and tie in a bow on the outside of the card.

7. Add the greeting of your choice.

Café Retro

Invite a friend for a cup of java with this bold black-and-white café scene. A thoughtful message from you enhances any social occasion.

Card Size: 5 × 6½ inches

Materials

- Café Retro patterns (page 112)
- one 8½ × 11-inch sheet white card stock
- one 8½ × 11-inch sheet black card stock
- tracing paper

Tools

- scissors
- ruler
- glue
- fine-line black marker
- pencil

Instructions

1. Cut a piece of white card stock 6½ × 10 inches. Fold in half so the card measures 5 × 6½ inches and the fold is at the top.

2. Cut thirty-one ¾ × ¾-inch squares from the black card stock. Glue to the front of the card in a checkerboard pattern. Trim any overhang from the edges.

3. Use the patterns to cut all the café pieces from the black card stock and the white card stock. Using the photo and the patterns as guides, glue all the pieces to the front of the card.

4. Using the marker, add accents to the chairs, table, coffee cups, and vase.

5. Add the greeting of your choice.

Purple Passion

If you love purple, this card is for you. A striking vase of foam flowers is sure to delight that special someone.

Card Size: $4\frac{1}{4} \times 8\frac{1}{2}$ inches

Materials

- one $8\frac{1}{2} \times 11$-inch sheet white card stock
- one $8\frac{1}{2} \times 11$-inch sheet handmade paper in a neutral shade
- one $8\frac{1}{2} \times 11$-inch sheet lavender card stock
- one $8\frac{1}{2} \times 11$-inch sheet dark purple card stock
- scraps of yellow and purple foam

Tools

- scissors
- ruler
- glue
- flower punch

Instructions

1. Cut a piece of white card stock $8\frac{1}{2} \times 8\frac{1}{2}$ inches. Fold in half so the card measures $4\frac{1}{4} \times 8\frac{1}{2}$ inches and the fold is on the left side.

2. Cut a piece of handmade paper $3\frac{3}{8} \times 5\frac{5}{8}$ inches. Mount on lavender card stock, leaving a $\frac{1}{8}$-inch border. Mount on dark purple card stock, leaving a $\frac{1}{8}$-inch border.

3. Mount the completed image on the front of the card, $\frac{1}{8}$ inch from top and $\frac{1}{8}$ inch from each side.

4. Make an assortment of yellow and purple flowers using different sizes of flower punches. If you do not have flower punches, draw or trace any flower pattern onto the foam and cut by hand. Arrange the flowers in an eye-catching design and glue to the handmade paper. (See photo.)

5. To make the flowerpot, cut a 2×4-inch piece of dark purple card stock. Roll into a cone shape until the top is slightly wider than the bottom. Glue to the card without folding flat. That will allow the pot to remain somewhat round and three-dimensional. (See photo.)

6. Add the greeting of your choice.

Nature Collage

Have fun designing, creating, and personalizing this card. No two cards will be alike. Make it your own by choosing a variety of natural and dried elements.

Card Size: 5 × 7 inches

Materials

- one 8½ × 11-inch sheet white watercolor paper
- assorted potpourri pieces and leaves
- one 4 × 6-inch sheet handmade green paper
- one 8½ × 11-inch sheet green card stock

Tools

- scissors
- ruler
- glue

Instructions

1. Cut a piece of white watercolor paper 7 × 10 inches. Fold in half so the card measures 5 × 7 inches and the fold is on the left side.

2. Select a variety of potpourri pieces and leaves and loosely arrange on the handmade paper. Move the items around until you find a pleasing arrangement of shapes and colors. Glue in place.

3. Mount on green card stock, trimming to leave a ⅛-inch border.

4. Mount the design, centered, on the front of the card.

5. Add the greeting of your choice.

Country Cabin

This colorful collage landscape will enchant the lucky recipient. Be creative when choosing the papers and make your card unique.

Card Size: 5 × 7 inches

Materials

- one 8½ × 11-inch sheet white card stock
- Country Cabin pattern (page 113)
- scraps of assorted papers
- tracing paper

Tools

- scissors
- ruler
- glue
- pencil

Instructions

1. Cut a piece of white card stock 7 × 10 inches. Fold in half so the card measures 5 × 7 inches and the fold is at the top.

2. Use the patterns to cut out the pieces of the picture. You might want to try specialty papers, such as clouds, mountains, leaves, grass, and flowers. If those are not available, substitute any printed or solid paper. Vary prints and solids for interesting contrasts.

3. When all the pieces are cut, lay them out to be sure you are satisfied with the arrangement. Glue in place.

4. Add the greeting of your choice.

Birthday Bouquet

This bouquet adds a special bloom to any birthday. Create a unique arrangement that will invite the recipient to stop and smell the flowers.

Card Size: $4\frac{1}{2} \times 6$ inches

Materials

- one $8\frac{1}{2} \times 11$-inch sheet white card stock
- one $8\frac{1}{2} \times 11$-inch sheet purple dotted paper
- one $8\frac{1}{2} \times 11$-inch sheet pink dotted paper
- one $8\frac{1}{2} \times 11$-inch sheet vellum

Tools

- scissors
- ruler
- glue
- flower rubber stamp
- markers

Instructions

1. Cut a piece of white card stock 6×9 inches. Fold in half so the card measures $4\frac{1}{2} \times 6$ inches and the fold is on the left side.

2. Cover the inside of the card with the pink dotted paper.

3. Cover the front of the card with the purple dotted paper.

4. Cut a piece of vellum $4\frac{1}{2} \times 6$ inches. Stamp the flower image slightly below center, leaving room for a greeting above the image. Color with markers and let dry thoroughly.

5. Glue the completed image to front of the card over the purple dotted paper.

6. Add the greeting of your choice.

Summer's Harvest

This card is sure to bring a smile to any gardener's face. You can personalize the card by selecting the recipient's favorite fruit or vegetable. Change the color scheme to complement the chosen food.

Card Size: 5 × 6½ inches

Materials

- one 8½ × 11-inch sheet medium brown card stock
- one 8½ × 11-inch sheet reddish orange paper
- light pink embossing powder
- small piece white card stock

Tools

- scissors
- ruler
- small swirl rubber stamp
- black stamp pad or marker
- clear embossing pad
- embossing gun
- glue
- tomato rubber stamp
- assorted markers

Instructions

1. Cut a piece of medium brown card stock 6½ × 10 inches. Fold in half so the card measures 5 × 6½ inches and the fold is on the left side.

2. Cut a piece of reddish orange paper 4¾ × 6⅛ inches. Stamp small swirls all over the paper and emboss with light pink embossing powder. (See page 20, "Embossing.") If you do not have a swirl stamp, you can draw your own swirl design with an embossing pen and then emboss.

3. Cut a window measuring 2 × 2½ inches. Place the window 1 inch down from the top and 1½ inches in from each side.

4. Stamp the tomato image on a small piece of white card stock and trim to size, about 2 × 2½ inches. Color the image with markers, using the photo as a guide.

5. Mount on a small piece of reddish orange paper, leaving a ⅛-inch border. Glue to inside of card so that the image shows through the window when the card is closed.

6. Add the greeting of your choice.

A Special Day

A wonderful birthday is almost guaranteed when this bright and bold greeting arrives in the mail.

Card Size: 5 × 6½ inches

Materials

- one 8½ × 11-inch sheet white card stock
- one 8½ × 11-inch sheet dotted paper
- one 8½ × 11-inch sheet yellow card stock
- Special Day patterns (page 114)
- one 8½ × 11-inch sheet black paper
- scraps of colored foam
- birthday candle stickers
- tracing paper

Tools

- scissors
- ruler
- glue
- gold marker
- pencil

Instructions

1. Cut a piece of white card stock 6½ × 10 inches. Fold in half so the card measures 5 × 6½ inches and the fold is on the left side.

2. Cover the front of the card with the dotted paper.

3. Cut a piece of yellow card stock 4¼ × 5½ inches and glue it, centered, to the front of the card.

4. Use the patterns to cut the shapes from black paper and glue to the yellow card stock. (See photo for placement.)

5. Use the patterns to cut the balloons and cake from foam. Use any colors of foam you like. Glue in place, using the photo as a guide.

6. Place the candle stickers on top of the birthday cake. If stickers are not available, make your own, using a rubber stamp (see page 23, "Using Stickers"), or cut pictures of candles from a magazine or coloring book.

7. Using the gold marker, draw a string on each balloon. (See photo.)

8. Add the greeting of your choice.

New England Afternoon

*Share a captivating view of quaint New England.
Cloud-printed paper creates the blue afternoon sky.
What a charming way to send your thoughts!*

Card Size: 5 × 7 inches

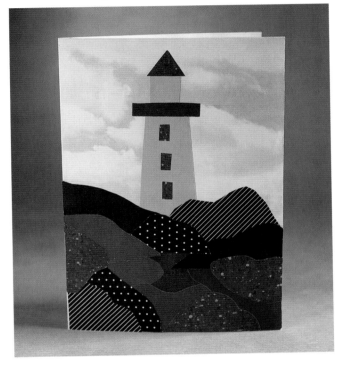

Materials

- one 8½ × 11-inch sheet white card stock
- New England Afternoon pattern (page 115)
- assorted papers
- tracing paper

Tools

- scissors
- ruler
- glue
- pencil

Instructions

1. Cut a piece of white card stock 7 × 10 inches. Fold in half so the card measures 5 × 7 inches and the fold is on the left side.

2. Select interesting scraps of paper and use the patterns to cut out the pieces. You can purchase cloud paper to use for the sky or cut out your own clouds and glue them on blue paper. Use a variety of patterns and solids for a balanced look.

3. When you've cut all the pieces and are happy with the arrangement, glue to the front of the card.

4. Add the greeting of your choice.

Sunflower Surprise

Gentle pastel shades enhance a perfect sunflower to mark any occasion and convey so many greetings: birthday, anniversary, get well, cheer up, hello, or I miss you.

Card Size: 5 × 6½ inches

Materials

- one 8½ × 11-inch sheet white card stock
- one 8½ × 11-inch sheet green checked paper
- one 8½ × 11-inch sheet tan card stock
- one 8½ × 11-inch sheet cream card stock
- one 8½ × 11-inch sheet dark green card stock

Tools

- scissors
- ruler
- glue
- sunflower rubber stamp
- brown stamp pad or marker
- makeup applicators, cotton swabs, or cotton balls
- pastels or chalk

Instructions

1. Cut a piece of white card stock 6½ × 10 inches. Fold in half so the card measures 5 × 6½ inches and the fold is on the left side.

2. Cover the front of the card with green checked paper.

3. Stamp the sunflower image on the tan card stock. Using a makeup applicator, cotton swab, or cotton ball, lightly rub on a pastel to pick up a small amount of color. Gently apply the color to the sunflower. Be careful not to overcolor. Repeat with other colors.

4. Mount on cream card stock, trimming to leave a ⅛-inch border.

5. Mount on dark green card stock, leaving a ⅛-inch border.

6. Center and mount on the front of the card.

7. Add the greeting of your choice.

Let It Snow

A jolly snowman says "Season's Greetings" in this happy holiday card.
Be creative with the hat and scarf; you're sure to draw a chuckle or two.

Card Size: 5 × 7 inches

Materials

- one 8½ × 11-inch sheet white card stock
- one 8½ × 11-inch sheet blue vellum
- scrap paper in a variety of patterns and colors, including brown and black
- 20 inches of blue ribbon
- Let It Snow patterns (page 116)
- tracing paper

Tools

- scissors
- ruler
- snowflake rubber stamp
- blue stamp pad or marker
- rectangular hole punch
- corrugator
- glue
- blue, black, and orange markers
- pencil

Instructions

1. Cut a piece of white card stock 7 × 10 inches. Fold in half so the card measures 5 × 7 inches and the fold is on the left side.

2. Open the card and lay it flat. With the blue stamp pad or marker, stamp the snowflake image so it covers the entire front and back of the card. Let it dry thoroughly.

3. Cut a piece of blue vellum 7 × 10 inches and fold in half. Place over card and punch two rectangular holes in the fold of the card, ½ inch from the top and ½ inch from the bottom. Be sure to punch through both the card and vellum layers.

4. String the blue ribbon through the holes and tie a bow on the outside of the card.

5. Use the patterns to cut out the pieces of the snowman. Use white card stock for the body, black paper for the hat, brown paper for the arms, and any complementary color or pattern for the hatband and scarf. Corrugate the body of the snowman. (See Chapter 2.)

6. Using the photo as a guide, glue the pieces in place.

7. With black marker, make dots for the mouth and buttons. With blue marker, make dots for the eyes. With orange marker, draw a carrot nose.

8. Add the greeting of your choice.

Sun Kiss

Send a little sunshine to brighten someone's day. Three flowers pop up from this sunny card.

Card Size: 5¾ × 6⅜ inches

Materials

- one 12 × 12-inch sheet white card stock
- one 8½ × 11-inch sheet dark green card stock
- one 8½ × 11-inch sheet yellow card stock

Tools

- scissors
- ruler
- glue
- flower rubber stamp
- dark red, orange, and green markers

Instructions

1. Cut a piece of white card stock 6⅜ × 11½ inches. Fold in half so the card measures 5¾ × 6⅜ inches and the fold is on the left side.

2. Cover the front of the card with the dark green card stock. Cut a piece of yellow card stock 5½ × 6 inches, center on dark green card front, and glue.

3. Cut a piece of white card stock 3¾ × 4 inches.

4. Using markers, color directly onto the rubber stamp: red for the petals, orange in the center, and green on the stem and leaves. Work quickly and stamp the image three times on the white card stock, re-inking the stamp after each impression.

5. Mount on yellow card stock, trimming to leave a ⅛-inch border.

6. Mount on green card stock, leaving a ⅛-inch border.

7. Center and mount on the front of the card.

8. Add the greeting of your choice.

Advanced-Level Projects

With beginner and intermediate levels completed, you are now ready for more advanced projects. The cards in this section are the most difficult in the book. They require more techniques, have more steps, and take more time to complete. Ready for the challenge? Let's go!

Shades of Roses

Stark black and white provide an elegant background for these colorful roses—perfect for any occasion. Scratch a lot or a little to reveal the colors underneath.

Card Size: 5 × 6½ inches

Materials

- two 8½ × 11-inch sheets white card stock
- one 5 × 7-inch sheet black scratch paper
- gold embossing powder
- one 8½ × 11-inch sheet black card stock

Tools

- scissors
- ruler
- flower rubber stamp, approximately 2½ × 4 inches
- clear embossing pad
- embossing gun
- wood stylus or another pointed wooden tool (for scratching)
- glue

Instructions

1. Cut a piece of white card stock 6½ × 10 inches. Fold the card in half so it measures 5 × 6½ inches and the fold is at the top. If you choose a larger rubber stamp, you may have to make your card larger.

2. Stamp the flower image on the black scratch paper, using the embossing pad. Sprinkle with gold embossing powder and emboss with the gun. (See page 20, "Embossing.") Cut evenly around the image, leaving about a ¼-inch border. (See photo.)

3. Using the stylus, carefully scratch the black from the petals and leaves so that the color of the scratch paper shows through.

4. Mount on white card stock, trimming to leave a ⅛-inch border. Mount on black card stock, leaving a ⅛-inch border. Mount on white card stock again, leaving a ⅛-inch border. Mount on black card stock again, leaving a ⅛-inch border. Center and mount on the front of the card.

5. Add the greeting of your choice.

Winter Green

Two trees are better than one. Hidden inside this card is another holiday tree just waiting to pop out. Surprise those special friends for the holidays.

Card Size: 5 x 6½ inches

Materials

- one 8½ × 11-inch sheet white card stock
- Winter Green patterns (page 117)
- two 8½ × 11-inch sheets green card stock
- one 8½ × 11-inch sheet printed vellum
- tracing paper

Tools

- scissors
- ruler
- glue
- small ornament rubber stamp
- red, blue, and green markers
- pencil

Instructions

1. Cut a piece of white card stock 6½ × 10 inches. Fold in half so the card measures 5 × 6½ inches and the fold is on the left side.

2. Use the pattern to cut the tree for the front of the card from green card stock. Center the tree on the front of the card and glue.

3. Fold the other sheet of card stock five times in an accordion pattern. Place the half-tree pattern on top of the folded card stock and cut it out. Be sure the branches are on the folds. Do not cut the folds. Open the folded paper and you will see three trees side by side, connected at the branches. Glue to the inside of the card. Attach the left half of the first tree to the inside left of the card, against the centerfold. Attach the right side of the third tree to the inside right of the card, against the centerfold. The tree will open and close with the card.

4. Cut a piece of vellum 6½ × 10 inches and fold in half. Glue over the front and back of card.

5. Using the small ornament stamp and markers, stamp the image on the vellum so the ornaments appear to hang on the tree.

6. Add the greeting of your choice.

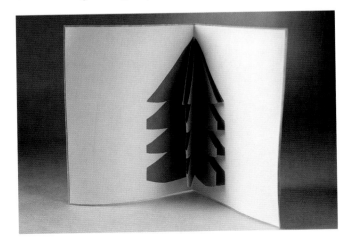

Flower Power

Celebrate a birthday or any festive occasion with a groovy statement. Give this three-dimensional card as many layers as you like.

Card Size: 5½ x 5½ inches

Materials

- one 8½ × 11-inch sheet bright blue card stock
- one 8½ × 11-inch sheet white card stock
- one 8½ × 11-inch sheet turquoise card stock

Tools

- scissors
- ruler
- large patterned rubber stamp
- black stamp pad or black marker
- assorted markers
- glue
- craft knife
- double-sided foam tape

Instructions

1. Cut a piece of bright blue card stock 5½ × 11 inches. Fold in half so the card measures 5½ × 5½ inches. The fold can be either at the top or on the left side, whichever you prefer.

2. Stamp the large patterned image on the white card stock. Color the design with markers.

3. Depending on the pattern you selected, cut the image into two or three pieces. Use the craft knife to cut the middle section(s) from the outside section. Mount the outside piece on turquoise card stock, leaving a ⅛-inch border. Mount this piece on the front of the card. Trim the blue card front from the inside of the image, leaving a window to the inside of the card.

4. Glue the additional sections(s) of the image to the inside of the card so each shows through the window when the card is closed. If you have two sections, glue one flat and raise the other with double-sided foam tape. (See photo.)

5. Add the greeting of your choice.

Nautical Watchtower

Quiet and serene is the mood of this lighthouse setting. It's a gentle way of letting people know they're in your thoughts.

Card Size: 5½ x 5 inches

Materials

- one 8½ × 11-inch sheet of turquoise card stock
- one 8½ × 11-inch sheet of watercolor paper
- one 8½ × 11-inch sheet of dark blue card stock

Tools

- scissors
- ruler
- lighthouse rubber stamp
- black marker
- watercolor pencils
- corner punch
- blender pen
- glue

Instructions

1. Cut a piece of turquoise card stock 5 × 11 inches. Fold in half so the card measures 5½ × 5 inches and the fold is at the top.

2. Cut a piece of watercolor paper 3⅝ × 4¼ inches. Using the black marker, stamp the lighthouse on the watercolor paper and let it dry thoroughly. Use the watercolor pencils and blender pen to color the image. (See page 22, "Watercolor Pencils.")

3. Cut a piece of dark blue card stock 3⅞ × 4½ inches. Using a corner punch on all four corners, make decorative slits to hold the lighthouse image in place. Center and mount on the front of the card.

4. Cut ⅛-inch strips from the dark blue card stock. Using the photo for placement, glue the strips to form a frame around the lighthouse.

5. Add the greeting of your choice.

Summer Garden

Beautiful birdhouses adorn this beguiling garden. Send this to the bird or gardening enthusiast on your list.

Card Size: 5½ x 6½ inches

Materials

- one 8½ × 11-inch sheet dark green card stock
- one 8½ × 11-inch sheet watercolor paper

Tools

- scissors
- ruler
- leaf rubber stamp
- watermark stamp pad
- flower rubber stamp
- brown marker
- watercolor pencils
- craft knife
- blender pen

Instructions

1. Cut a piece of dark green card stock 6½ × 11 inches. Fold in half so the card measures 5½ × 6½ inches and the fold is on the left side.

2. Using the watermark stamp pad and the leaf stamp, cover the front of the card with leaf images. (See page 19, "Using Rubber Stamps.")

3. Stamp the flower image on the watercolor paper, using the brown marker. Let it dry thoroughly. Color with watercolor pencils and the blender pen. Trim the image to 3⅝ × 5⅛ inches. Adjust the size if your rubber stamp is larger or smaller.

4. Cut four diagonal slits in the front of the card (see photo) and slip the watercolor into them.

5. Add the greeting of your choice.

Psychedelic Splash

Go your own way with this one. You choose what to color and how to layer this captivating design reminiscent of 1960s psychedelia. Personalize it for a special way of remembering any occasion.

Card Size: 5 x 6½ inches

Materials

- two 8½ × 11-inch sheets white card stock
- one 8½ × 11-inch sheet bright pink card stock
- one 8½ × 11-inch sheet dark purple card stock

Tools

- scissors
- ruler
- large collage rubber stamp
- black stamp pad or black marker
- markers of various colors
- glue
- craft knife
- double-sided foam tape

Instructions

1. Cut a piece of white card stock 6½ × 10 inches. Fold in half so the card measures 5 × 6½ inches and the fold is on the left side.

2. Stamp the collage image, using a black stamp pad or marker, on the remaining piece of white card stock. Let it dry thoroughly. Highlight areas of the stamped image with colored markers. Do not color everything. The design will be more striking if some parts are in black and white.

3. Choose a few sections of the collage to cut out. (You will raise them later with foam tape.) Set aside.

4. Mount the colored image on a piece of bright pink card stock, trimming to leave a ⅛-inch border. Mount again on dark purple card stock, leaving a ⅛-inch border. Center and mount on the front of the card.

Choose a section to show through a window in the card and cut it out with the craft knife. Glue the section to the inside of the card so it shows through the window.

5. Use the double-sided tape to attach the reserved sections to the front of the card.

6. When your card is closed, your collage will have three layers: the piece glued flat to the card front, the raised sections, and the piece showing through the window.

7. Add the greeting of your choice.

Old Saint Nick

Tradition abounds in this old-time Santa image. Hand-painted in acrylics, Santa comes in his own picture frame and is ready to display on the mantel above the stockings.

Card Size: 5½ x 7¼ inches

Materials

- one 8½ × 11-inch sheet dark green card stock
- Old Saint Nick pattern (page 118)
- Frame Stand pattern (page 121)
- one 4 × 5-inch canvas
- transfer paper
- one sheet green foam
- one 8½ × 11-inch sheet dark green corrugated paper
- tracing paper
- graphite paper

Tools

- scissors
- ruler
- pencil
- acrylic paints
- paintbrushes
- glue
- craft knife
- pencil
- wood stylus

Instructions

1. Cut a piece of dark green card stock 7¼ × 11 inches. Fold in half so the card measures 5½ × 7¼ inches and the fold is on the left side.

2. Transfer the Santa pattern to the canvas (see Chapter 1), and paint with acrylic paints.

3. Cut a 5½ × 7¼-inch piece of green foam and glue to the front of the card.

4. Cut a piece of dark green corrugated paper 5½ × 7¼ inches. Using a craft knife, cut a hole the size of the canvas out of the center. Glue on top of the foam.

5. Glue the painted Santa canvas inside the opening in the corrugated paper.

6. From the remaining corrugated paper, cut a piece 4 × 5 inches. Use the pattern and a craft knife to cut the frame stand. Glue it inside the front of the card. Be sure not to glue the flap; you want it to open and close freely.

7. Add the greeting of your choice.

Stained-Glass Window

Try this elegant way of saying "Happy Easter." Stained-glass windows, matted and ready for framing, will gladden anyone who celebrates this special spring holiday.

Card Size: 5 x 6½ inches

Materials

- two 8½ × 11-inch sheets white card stock
- one 5 × 7-inch sheet black scratch paper
- gold embossing powder

Tools

- scissors
- ruler
- two window rubber stamps
- clear embossing pad
- embossing gun
- wood stylus
- glue
- craft knife

Instructions

1. Cut a piece of white card stock 6½ × 10 inches. Fold in half so the card measures 5 × 6½ inches and the fold is at the top.

2. Using a clear embossing pad and gold embossing powder, emboss the two window images on black scratch paper. (See page 20, "Embossing.") If you have only one window stamp, either stamp the same window twice or turn the card lengthwise and use only one window.

3. Scratch out the design with the wood stylus until no black remains. You will have a gold-embossed out-line with the colors showing through, giving the look of stained glass. Glue to the front of the card. (See photo.)

4. Cut a piece of white card stock 5 × 6½ inches. Cut two openings—the size of the windows—in the card stock with a craft knife. Glue over the windows so they are framed by the openings.

5. Add the greeting of your choice.

Butterfly Dream

Colorful tissue paper provides the background for this glorious collage. Vellum butterflies change color with the tissue paper.

Card Size: 5 x 6½ inches

Materials

- one 8½ × 11-inch sheet white card stock
- scraps of colored tissue paper
- one 8½ × 11-inch sheet clear vellum
- one 8½ × 11-inch laminating sheet

Tools

- scissors
- ruler
- glue
- assorted butterfly rubber stamps
- black marker
- permanent markers in various colors
- craft knife

Instructions

1. Cut a piece of white card stock 6½ × 10 inches. Fold in half so the card measures 5 × 6½ inches and the fold is on the left side.

2. Tear the tissue paper into small, irregularly shaped pieces. Vary the sizes and colors. Glue randomly to the front of the card.

3. Using the black marker and butterfly stamps, stamp a variety of images on the sheet of clear vellum. Set it aside and allow it to dry thoroughly. When it is dry, use permanent markers to color in the butterflies. Carefully cut out the images with a craft knife and glue on top of the tissue paper. If you prefer, use butterfly stickers in place of this step.

4. Place the laminating sheet over the card to seal the tissue paper and butterflies. With the craft knife, trim the excess flush with the edges of the card.

5. Add the greeting of your choice.

Under the Sea

Say it with fish. These multicolored, embossed fish are just right for any occasion—or no occasion at all.

Card Size: 5 x 7 inches

Materials

- one 8½ × 11-inch sheet blue card stock
- one 8½ × 11-inch sheet white card stock
- clear embossing powder
- one 8½ × 11-inch sheet turquoise card stock
- one 8½ × 11-inch sheet dark blue card stock

Tools

- scissors
- ruler
- multicolor blue stamp pad
- assorted fish rubber stamps
- embossing gun
- glue
- double-sided foam tape

Instructions

1. Cut a piece of blue card stock 7 × 10 inches. Fold in half so the card measures 5 × 7 inches and the fold is at the top.

2. Using the fish stamps and the multicolor blue stamp pad, stamp five or six fish images on the white card stock. Cover with clear embossing powder and heat with the embossing gun. (See page 20, "Embossing.")

3. Cut out the fish images. Mount each on turquoise card stock, trimming to leave a ⅛-inch border. Mount each on dark blue card stock, leaving a ⅛-inch border. Using the photo as a guide, arrange and glue some of the fish flat to the front of the card. Save one fish to attach with the double-sided tape for a raised look.

4. Add the greeting of your choice.

Perfect Poinsettias

Embossed poinsettias are classic, perfect for adding color and cheer to the holidays. Send them to everyone on your list.

Card Size: 5 x 6½ inches

Materials

- two 8½ × 11-inch sheets white card stock
- clear embossing powder
- one 8½ × 11-inch sheet green card stock
- one 8½ × 11-inch red card stock

Tools

- scissors
- ruler
- poinsettia rubber stamp
- green marker
- red and green embossing markers
- embossing gun
- glue

Instructions

1. Cut a piece of white card stock 6½ × 10 inches. Fold in half so the card measures 5 × 6½ inches and the fold is at the top.

2. Stamp the poinsettia image on white card stock, using a green marker. Let it dry thoroughly. Using the red embossing marker, color one flower at a time. Apply clear embossing powder and heat with the gun. Repeat the procedure, using the green embossing marker on the leaves. Work on one small area at a time so the ink does not dry too quickly. (See page 20, "Embossing.")

3. Trim the edges of the embossed image and mount on green card stock, trimming to leave a ⅛-inch border. Mount on red card stock, leaving a ⅛-inch border. Center and mount the completed image on the front of the card.

4. Add the greeting of your choice.

Nature's Beauty

Mix and match embellishments galore. Make it your way. Personalize it by varying the flowers and changing the colors.

Card Size: 5 x 7 inches

Materials

- one 8½ × 11-inch sheet watercolor paper
- one 8½ × 11-inch sheet tan card stock
- one 8½ × 11-inch sheet handmade paper in a neutral shade
- silk butterfly
- assorted silk flowers

Tools

- scissors
- ruler
- glue
- gold metallic marker

Instructions

1. Cut a piece of watercolor paper 7 × 10 inches. Fold in half so the card measures 5 × 7 inches and the fold is on the left side.

2. Cut a 4¼ × 4¼-inch square of tan card stock and glue in the center of the card. Outline the square with the gold marker.

3. Cut a 4 × 4-inch square of the handmade paper and glue diagonally on top of tan card stock square. (See photo.) Outline the square with the gold marker.

4. Arrange the butterfly and the flowers on the front of the card and glue in place.

5. Add the greeting of your choice.

Matching Gift Tag

1. Cut a piece of white card stock 3 × 6 inches. Fold in half so the tag measures 3 × 3 inches. The fold can be either on the side or at the top.

2. Cut a 2 × 2-inch square of tan card stock and glue to the tag. Outline the square with the gold marker.

3. Cut a 1¾ × 1¾-inch square of the handmade paper and glue diagonally on top of the tan card stock. Outline the square with the gold marker.

4. Glue a matching flower or butterfly to the center of the tag.

Teatime

Let them know it's time for a tea party. This gold embossed card is perfect to say "I miss you and it's time to get together."

Card Size: 5 x 7 inches

Materials

- one 8½ × 11-inch sheet light tan card stock
- one 8½ × 11-inch sheet brown card stock
- gold embossing powder
- one 8½ × 11-inch sheet cream card stock
- one 8½ × 11-inch sheet dark tan card stock

Tools

- scissors
- ruler
- teacup rubber stamp
- teapot rubber stamp
- clear embossing pad
- embossing gun
- glue

Instructions

1. Cut a piece of light tan card stock 7 × 10 inches. Fold in half so the card measures 5 × 7 inches and the fold is on the left side.

2. On the brown card stock, stamp and emboss in gold the teacup and teapot images. (See page 20, "Embossing.") Trim the images.

3. Mount each image on cream card stock, trimming to leave a ⅛-inch border. Mount each again on dark tan card stock, leaving a ⅛-inch border.

4. Glue the images onto the front of the card. (See photo for placement.)

5. Add the greeting of your choice.

Spring Day

A garden of watercolor jewels is just right for a birthday, Mother's Day, or any day you want to make someone feel special.

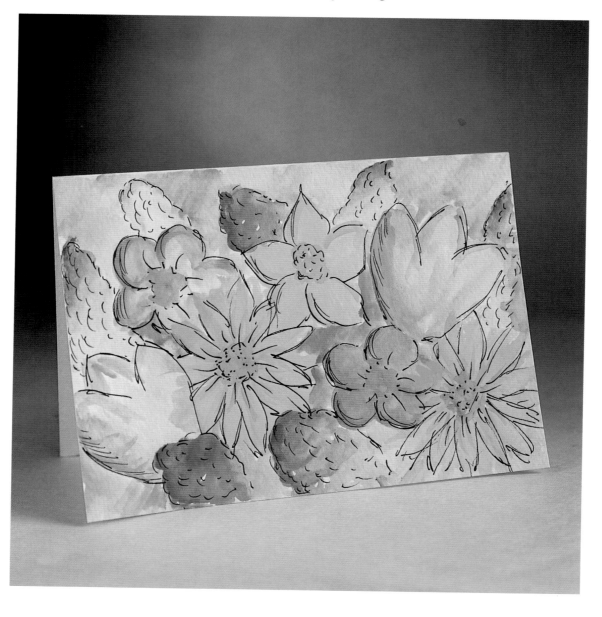

Card Size: 5 x 7 inches

Materials

- one $8\frac{1}{2} \times 11$-inch sheet white watercolor paper
- Spring Day pattern (page 119)
- graphite paper
- tracing paper

Tools

- scissors
- ruler
- pencil
- watercolors
- paintbrushes
- black fine-line marker
- wood stylus

Instructions

1. Cut a piece of white watercolor paper 7×10 inches. Fold in half so the card measures 5×7 inches and the fold is at the top.

2. Transfer the pattern to the front of the card. (See Chapter 1.) Using the photo as a guide, paint the flowers with watercolors.

3. Using the photo as a guide, outline and accent flowers with the black marker.

4. Add the greeting of your choice.

Quiet Time

For those reflective or nostalgic times, convey your feelings with the image of a solitary child.

Card Size: 5 x 6½ inches

Materials

- one 8½ × 11-inch sheet blue card stock
- one 8½ × 11-inch sheet dark blue card stock
- one 8½ × 11-inch sheet white card stock

Tools

- scissors
- ruler
- craft knife
- glue
- little-girl rubber stamp
- black marker
- watercolor pencils
- blender pen

Instructions

1. Cut a piece of blue card stock 6½ × 10 inches. Fold in half so the card measures 5 × 6½ inches and the fold is on the left side.

2. Use the craft knife to cut a 2½ × 2½-inch square window, 1¼ inches from the top and 1¼ inches from each side.

3. Cut ¼-inch strips of dark blue card stock. Using the photo for placement, glue to the card.

4. Stamp the little-girl image with a black marker on white card stock. Let it dry thoroughly. Lightly color with watercolor pencils and the blender pen. Mount on a piece of dark blue card stock, leaving a ⅛-inch border. Glue to the inside of the card so the image shows through the window when the card is closed.

5. Add the greeting of your choice.

Pumpkin Patch

Have some fun with this project and fill the pumpkin patch. This card doubles as a Halloween decoration, complete with its own stand.

Card Size: 5½ x 5½ inches

Materials

- one 8½ × 11-inch sheet black card stock
- one 8½ × 11-inch sheet orange card stock
- one 8½ × 11-inch sheet yellow card stock
- one 8½ × 11-inch laminating sheet
- Pumpkin Patch patterns (page 120)
- Frame Stand pattern (page 121)
- tracing paper
- graphite paper

Tools

- scissors
- ruler
- craft knife
- glue
- ghost foam stamp
- white paint
- pencil
- stylus

Instructions

1. Cut a piece of black card stock 5½ × 11 inches. Using the pattern as a guide, fold on the lines to form the card.

2. Cut ten pumpkins from orange card stock and ten pumpkins from yellow card stock. Cut faces in the orange pumpkins.

3. Match the orange and yellow pumpkins and glue the orange pumpkins on top of the yellow pumpkins. Using the photo as a guide, glue the pumpkins to the card.

4. With the ghost stamp and white paint, stamp the image on a scrap of black card stock. Allow to dry thoroughly. Cover with the laminating sheet and trim around the edges with the craft knife. Stick the ghost to top right corner of the card. (See photo.) If you prefer, use a ghost sticker in place of this step.

5. Cut the frame stand from black card stock, using the pattern and the craft knife. Glue to the back of the card, leaving the flap free to support the card.

6. Add the greeting of your choice.

His and Hers

Rag dolls make a cute anniversary wish for that special couple. Use any boy and girl stamps, and change the colors to suit your preference.

Card Size: 5 x 6½ inches

Materials

- one 8½ × 11-inch sheet white card stock
- one 8½ × 11-inch sheet red-and-white checked paper
- black embossing powder
- one 8½ × 11-inch sheet red card stock
- one 8½ × 11-inch sheet yellow-orange card stock

Tools

- scissors
- ruler
- boy and girl rubber stamps
- clear embossing pad
- embossing gun
- assorted markers
- glue

Instructions

1. Cut a piece of white card stock 6½ × 10 inches. Fold in half so the card measures 5 × 6½ inches and the fold is at the top. Cover the front of the card with the checked paper.

2. Emboss the boy and girl images on white card stock and trim square. (See page 20, "Embossing.") Color with markers. Mount on red card stock, trimming to leave a ⅛-inch border around each image.

3. Mount both images on a piece of yellow-orange card stock, leaving a ¼-inch border around each image. (See photo.) Mount on red card stock, leaving a ⅛-inch border. Center and mount the completed image on the card.

4. Add the greeting of your choice.

CHAPTER SEVEN

Greetings

Choosing a greeting appropriate for the occasion is an important step in making any card.

Once you have selected a greeting, you will need to transfer it to the card. Using tracing paper and the greetings and alphabets provided, trace the greeting onto the tracing paper. Position the paper on your project and lightly tape it down so it will not move. Slide a sheet of graphite paper under the tracing paper, graphite side down. Use a stylus or pencil and lightly—and carefully—trace over the letters. This will leave a light impression on your card. Choose a marker and go over the traced greeting on your card.

If you are placing the greeting on vellum, just put the greeting underneath the vellum and trace. No graphite is needed. Vellum greetings can be used over most designs if you prefer.

Rubber stamps are an excellent source for greetings and sayings, and they are easy to use. Just ink and stamp your greeting wherever you want it.

Use stickers to create greetings. They are available in many colors, sizes, and designs. It is as simple as peel and stick. Lightly pencil in guidelines to line up the letters. No transferring is necessary.

If you feel adventurous, try to hand-letter your own greetings. Practice on scrap paper until you are satisfied. Experiment with different pens. Calligraphy pens can make decorative writing easy.

You can find alphabets, letters, and sayings in many places, such as magazines, coloring books, old greeting cards, and books. Clip out sayings to use later. Always be on the lookout for fresh material and ideas.

In Appendix B, "Lettering," you'll find an alphabet that can be used for any project in this book. You can also use a word-processing program—just find a font you like, type your message, print it, and transfer it to your project.

Patterns

Rose Garden

Festive Announcement

Festival of Color

Café Retro

Country Cabin

A Special Day

New England Afternoon

Let It Snow

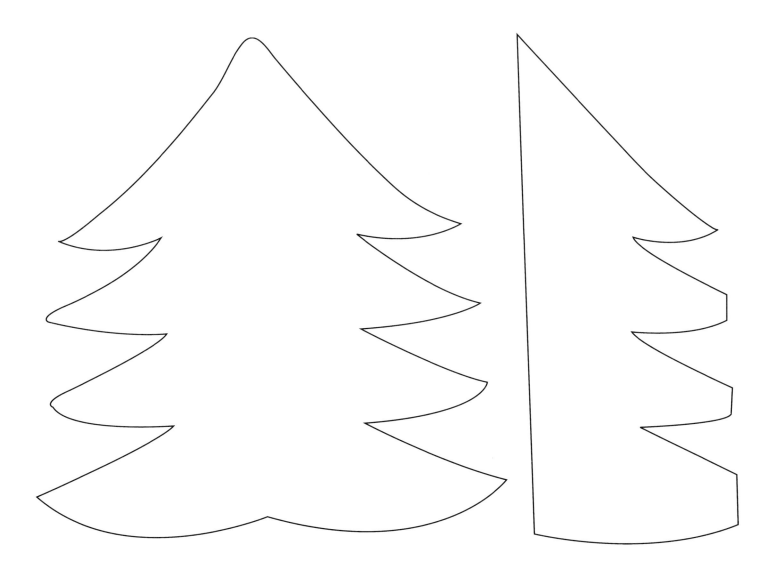

Winter Green

Old Saint Nick
See page 121 for stand pattern.

Spring Day

cut 1

cut 2

cut 1

cut 3

cut 1

cut 2

Pumpkin Patch

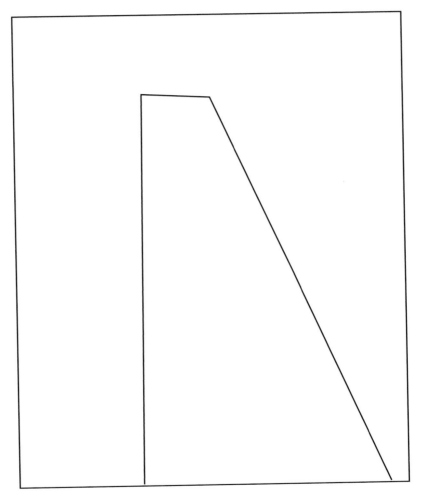

stand pattern

Lettering

Aa Bb Cc Dd

Ee Ff Gg Hh

Ii Jj Kk Ll

Mm Nn Oo

Pp Qq Rr Ss

Tt Uu Vv Ww

Xx Yy Zz

1 2 3 4 5

6 7 8 9 0

st nd rd th

Happy Birthday

Anniversary

Valentine's Day

Mother's Day

Father's Day

Merry Christmas

Hanukkah

New Year

Brunch

BBQ

Graduation

You're Invited

Bon Voyage

Best Wishes

Thinking of You

Baby Shower

Bridal Shower

4th of July

With Sympathy

Party

Celebrate

Cocktail Party

Happiness

Wedding Wishes

Your Special Day

Sorry for Your Loss

Thinking of

It's a

Boy

Girl

Index